This is a Handbook guide for new authors who want to write a book and tell their story. I will give you insight as to how you start and finish your story as well as publish your own book!

Using these 8 simple steps…

Mike Warren

Copyright © 2015 by Mike Warren

Mike Warren Publishing

DEDICATION

To all of you who

Want to write their

Own story and

Have it published.

This book

Is for

YOU!!!

Mike Warren

CONTENTS

How do I write a book?

    A. What's your story?
    B. Write about what you know.
    C. K.I.S.S. = Keep It Simple Stupid
    D. Research
    E. First Person vs. Third Person
    F. Story teller vs. being a writer. What's interesting and what's not.

Word Count

    A. 10,000 to 25,000 (Short Story)
    B. 25,000 to 50,000 (Novella)
    C. 50,00 and above (Novel)

Sample Readers

    A. Read and re-read your manuscript for errors/mistakes.
    B. Always have 2 or 3 family/friends read your manuscript.

C. Always have 2 or 3 associates read your manuscript.

Finding an Editor

A. Where to find an Editor
B. Prices will vary depending on the expertise of the individual Editor.
C. Don't be afraid to shop around and compare prices.

Finding a Graphic Artist

A. Where to find a Graphic Artist
B. Ideas of what you want your book cover to look like.
C. Ebooks vs. Paperbacks or both.
D. Prices of Ebooks and Paperbacks.
E. Don't be afraid to shop around and compare prices.

Publish vs Self Publishing

A. The good
B. The bad
C. The ugly
D. ISBN's & ASIN's

Advertising

A. How to promote
B. Where to promote
C. Tools to promote

Copyrights

    A. What is Copyright
    B. Do I have to Copyright my book
    C. How much does it cost
    D. Where do I file for the Copyright of my book

The Reality of being an Author

    A. Should I quit my job
    B. Will I become rich and famous

PREFACE

For the past couple of years I have been teaching workshops for new authors on how to write and publish their own book, using just these 8 simple steps. As an Award Winning Author, people often come to me and ask, how do I get started? And I tell them, just write! Write whatever you want to write about just make sure you know what you're writing about. (Research)

Truth be told, avid readers make the best authors. It's funny, I come across so many people who say they want to write a book and I ask them, "So you like to read, huh?" and most of them say, "No, not really." And I look at them like, really, are you kidding me?

The reason I say avid readers make the best authors is because they have read so many books that they know how to make their book stand out. They seem to write their stories with an extra twist. Unlike some of these books that are just being rehash, if you know what I mean.

Because of today's economy so many things have changed when it comes to writing and publishing a book. When I first started writing my first book almost 10 years ago, I knew absolutely nothing about the writing world and what it took to get a book publish. I was so naïve that you probably know more than I did.

However, now is an exciting time to write that book and get it out into the masses for the world to read and it's easier and cheaper than you might think!

What if I told you that you could write your own book and publish it for less than $200 bucks?

Do I have your attention now? Good!

Let's begin…

Chapter 1

How do I write a book?

The first thing you have to do is decide what you want to write about. Is it your life story? Is it fiction or non-fiction? According to Webster dictionary, Fiction means, the class of literature comprising works of imaginative narration, especially in prose form. Non-fiction is, the branch of literature comprising works of narrative prose and dealing with or offering opinions or conjectures upon facts and reality, including biographies, history and essays.

As I mentioned earlier, write what you know. Don't try to write a story about the Moon or Mars if you've never been there. In essence, when you write a story about yourself or anything else, you have to become the expert and who knows more about your life story better than you? You are the expert. And be honest and truthful. Many times writers will skip over parts of their life that may still hurt them and therefore don't include it in their book. This will be a judgment call on your part. You have to decide whether or not it will be beneficial in telling your story. However, keep in mind that whatever pain or experience you've had to endure may help someone else that might be going through what you went through. Again, the decision is yours.

Who do you want to be your "TARGET" audience? In other words, who do you want to read your book? Every writer will answer this question by saying, "Everybody." Unfortunately, everybody won't read your book and everybody won't like what you might write about. But, that's par for the course of wanting to be an author. Before writing your book, take some time out and seriously think about whom you want your target audience to be.

Once you've made that decision, focus your book around them. Let's say you want a female audience…write your book to cater to females. Same for males, write your book to cater to males. Let's say your target group will be readers between the ages of 18 to 35…write your book to cater to them and so forth and so on. I hope you get my point.

The Right Way To Write Your Story

Many times, writers have a tendency in wanting to use "Big" 10 letter words to show off their knowledge of the English language. I try to impress upon new authors, please use everyday words, simple words that the average person can understand. Keep in mind, if you are writing your book for the masses, some Readers may only have a 6th grade education. There's nothing worse than trying to read a book and have to have a dictionary standing by. This is definitely a no no.

When writing your book, PLEASE, PLEASE, use the English language and not "EBONICS." Of course there's always an exception to every rule. The exception is, if there's a character speaking in quotes, Ebonics may be used. Example: "Yo ma dude, whatcha doin?" or "No dis muthafucka didn't!" The reason why this is acceptable is because you have to stay true to who the character is. Most likely, if your character is from the "Hood" and never graduated from high school, chances are he or she may speak that way. Even if your character is from the hood but they speak perfect English make sure they speak perfect English in their dialog.

When writing your book and if there is no dialog, make sure you write in perfect English as well as perfect grammar and syntax. Some new authors sometimes can't form or construct a simple sentence. I try to encourage new authors to take a writing course just so they can hone in their skill of writing. However, if you can't do that for whatever reason, don't despair, that's why you hire an Editor. I will discuss the hiring and the role of an Editor in chapter 4.

All writers will either write in first person or third person. First person example: "I couldn't believe what I was looking at." Third person example, "Joe couldn't believe what he was looking at." You see the difference? Personally, I enjoy writing in first person because Readers are able to understand what the character is feeling, thinking and saying. Whereas, when writing in third person, you have to try to express to the Readers what someone else is feeling, thinking and trying to say.

Now that you have the basics of starting a book, you now have to decide where and how you want to begin. There are several ways in starting a book:

1. Dialog…Characters are having a conversation with one another
2. A death scene…
3. A fight scene

4. A sex scene

Of course there are more but these startups are the most popular. The reason is, you want to catch Readers attention from the very first sentence of your book. Readers are busy people, they work, they have families, and most times they aren't patient enough to read a whole chapter before they decide whether or not to buy your book.

With that in mind, in story telling or writing a book, you have to decide what is interesting and what is not. Keep in mind, if you're telling your story and you write about how you and your homey went out one night at a bar and got pissy drunk. That's not interesting to a Reader. However, if you tell me that you and your homey went out at a bar, got pissy drunk but that's where you met the love of your life or a person that is relevant to your story, then that's fine. As a Reader, I would want to know where and how you met this person that is going to be relevant to your story.

Whatever you write about, make it relevant to your story because Readers will be able to understand what happened and where you're coming from. Thus allowing them (Readers) to enjoy what you're writing about.

Some writers will start their book with an outline. Example:

Chapter 1:

Chapter 2:

Chapter 3:

Very similar to this book that you're reading now. I'm using an outline format so that you as the reader will know what's in each chapter at the very beginning. However, this is not my style of writing. Normally, I think long and hard as to where I want to start my story and how I want it to end. For me, this is an easier method because as long as I know where I want to start my story and end my story, for all practical purposes, everything in between is just "Filler." In essence, I just need to get from point A to point Z.

Also, keep your chapters short and sweet. Some writers have a tendency to write long and drawn out chapters that may be 10 or so pages long. If you are one of these writers, that's up to you. However, studies have shown that when you write chapters that are short (4 or 7) pages long, the reader has the tendency in continuing reading even when they have told themselves that this is the last chapter and it's late and they have to get up in the morning for work. All it is, is a psychological thing. I don't know how many times Readers have emailed me or looked me up on facebook and have said, thanks to you and your book, I was late for work because I couldn't put your book down last night and go to sleep.

I know that might not be a nice thing to cause your Readers to be late for work or whatever but keeping your chapters short and sweet, it works.

When writing your book, do as much "Research" as you can. Even though it might be your life's story, make sure everything is accurate. The best tool for this is the internet. There are times where I can't spell the simplest word but as long as I have spell check and the dictionary website, it helps.

www.dictionary.reference.com

If you're writing a scene about a nightclub, a neighborhood, a restaurant, a city/town or even about a well known person, your best resource is:

www.goggle.com

Don't be afraid to use these websites, as a writer/author they will become your best friend.

Remember this….when writing your book, the standard industry practice is the font size of your words which should be at 12. In other words, always use the font size of 12.

Once you finish writing your book and if you want paperback copies of your book, you now have to write a synopsis for the back cover of your book. A synopsis is just a 5 or 6 sentence paragraph telling Readers what your book is about.

For me, I can write a book all day long but when it comes to writing the synopsis, this seems to be very difficult for me. But, I am getting better at it. lol

Chapter 2

Word Count

Many people ask me all the time, how important is word count? I tell them, it's very important because this will determine how short or how long your book will be. Word count will also determine what type of book it is. What I mean is, is it a short story? Is it a novella? Or is it a full length novel?

A. Short story word count.... 10,000 to 25,000 words
B. Novella word count……...25,000 to 50,000 words
C. Full length novel…………50,000 and above

I know it appears to be a lot of words but you will be surprise while writing your story how many words you use.

Some authors are very descriptive in their writing because they want to paint a picture for their Readers. You've heard of the expression, I like to be a fly on the wall when this happens or when that happens. Descriptive writing is a skill. You want to paint a picture in each scene you write about but, you have to be very careful. You don't want to overdo it because your book will become too wordy and therefore will bore your Readers.

Like I said, descriptive writing is a skill and the more you write, the better you become at it. It's called honing your skill. Even if you write 15, 20 or 30 novels you still can learn something new. A writer/author will always continue to learn the skill of descriptive writing.

The best way to keep track of your word count is simply look down at the bottom of your computer it will inform you as to what page number you're on and how many words you have written thus far.

Chapter 3

Sample Readers

Most writers/authors will have sample readers to read their work, mainly because they want feedback. My personal motto has always been the 3 E's.

1. Educate
2. Excite
3. Explain

The first is Educate, whatever you write about keep in mind, the Reader should always take away something that they didn't know before reading your book.

The second is Excite, whatever you write about keep in mind, you want your reader to be excited and interested in your story from the beginning to its ending.

The third is Explain, whatever you write about keep in mind you want your reader to understand exactly what you are trying to convey. Writing in first person as we talked about before makes this easier to do because the Reader understands exactly what you are feeling, thinking and trying to say.

So don't be embarrassed to have 2 or 3 of your friends or family members read your story. Once you publish your book, they're going to read it eventually. The reason for having sample readers is to get feedback. You want to know that whatever you write about, others will find it to be interesting as well. Now, in most cases, family and friends will generally try not to hurt your feelings and tell you they really enjoyed your story.

With that in mind, that's why it is also important to have 2 or 3 strangers/associates read your story as well. 9 times out of 10, they will be honest and tell you whether they liked it or not.

If you really want the God honest truth, there are professional sample readers out here that will sometimes do it for free and others will charge a small fee. Most of these professional sample readers can be found on social media. Whereas, facebook, instagram, and twitter. Like I said, they may charge you a small fee, anywhere from free to $50 bucks and up. But, before you pay someone else to read your work, first check with your teacher, co-worker, or just an associate of yours who you know enjoys reading.

Again, the reason for this is because you think your writing is interesting doesn't mean everyone else will. Remember, "Feedback" is very important. And just because someone doesn't find you work interesting doesn't mean that it's not. That's why as a writer, you want as many people, family/friends/associates and the like to read your writings and not just one person. Like the saying goes, the more, the merrier.

Chapter 4

Finding an Editor

Ok, let's say at this point, you have written your story and you have had several people read it and they all enjoyed it. Now, you're ready to publish it. **NOT...**

It's now time for you to find an Editor. The main misconception about Editors is that once you finish writing your book, the editor will make all corrections and re-write your book for you. **WRONG...**

An Editor's job is to merely point out misspelled words, grammatical errors, sentence structure and as the writer, you will make the changes. It's kind of like when you were in high school and Ms. English was your English teacher and you had to write a 5 page essay paper on what you did over the summer. Once you received your paper back and she highlighted the errors with her "Red" pen. She gave it back to you to make the corrections. This is the same with an Editor. He or she will highlight the errors in a PDF file and email your manuscript back to you.

I know most people think why should I pay an Editor so much money if they are not going to make these corrections? Well, the reason is, if the editor make these corrections and re-write your book the way it should be written, they would have to have a by-line.

A by-line is your name as the author and the Editor's name because they rewrote your book for you. So, they too will share in 50% of the profits from the sale of your book.

No writer/author wants to share a by-line if they can help it because it's your story. Why would you want to split half of your earnings with someone else?

AN EDITOR'S COST

Mike Warren

An Editor's fee/cost will vary from Editor to Editor. The rule of thumb is that most editors will charge $1.00 per page. See, this is where word count comes into play. The more words you have, the longer your book will be. Hence, if your book is 100 pages long, the cost for editing will be $100 bucks, 200 pages long, that's $200 bucks, so on and so on.

But don't let these prices scare you because once you get into this game of being an author/writer you begin to meet other authors, editors and the like. For example, I have a friend who has a Masters in English and even though Editing is not his fulltime job, he does my editing for $100 bucks regardless as to how long or short my book may be.

That being said, you might know someone who has a degree in English, maybe an English teacher, a friend, a co-worker. You will be surprise of the many people you might already know that is capable of editing your book for you for a small fee. Personally, I think $100 is a small fee and it is so worth it in the long run.

With that being said, everyone makes mistakes, we are only human and that also includes your Editor. As a writer, I have read my manuscripts many times as well as had several friends read my manuscripts but once my manuscript becomes a book, everybody and their momma will say, I saw this error or that error in your book. Truth of the matter is, we all make mistakes and the reality is, I have never read a book that didn't have an error in it.

I'm not trying to justify errors but it happens to the best of us. The only solution to minimize this problem is to read over your manuscript, friends/family read over your manuscript and pay an Editor to read over your manuscript. And once we decide to turn our manuscript into a finish product (book) hopefully the error(s) will be minimal and won't take away from the storyline.

Last but not least, I hope you have a tough skin because Readers will always find something wrong such as misspelled word(s) and/or grammar issues. Even though a Reader may have a problem with these issues, thank the Reader nonetheless because they took the time to buy and read your book. Remember, you are now a "Brand" and the last thing you want to do is piss your Readers off.

Chapter 5

Finding a Graphic Artist

After doing the writing, the editing etc...now it's time to decide what you want the cover of your book to look like.

Most writers/authors will do this in stages, write their book, have family and friends read their book, have an Editor edit their book and then decide on the cover.

Me, on the other hand, once I think of a story to write about, the first thing I do is have a book cover made by a Graphic Artist. I do this because once I have the cover of the book, I take a 4x6 photo of it and put it in a frame and set it on my desk (work station). As I'm writing the book, I can constantly look at the cover so that my story line will be focused on what my book cover looks like, if that makes sense?

The choice is yours to make. It's really up to you but for me, I prefer doing it my way. Just like you will determine what's best for you.

A Graphic Artist can make your book cover any way you want it to be. However, you have to educate your Graphic Artist as to what your book is about so they can have a better idea as to what you want your book cover to look like.

Most authors will want to have their leading character (s) on the book cover. People often ask me, where do you find your models and how much do they charge for a photo shoot.

Let me tell you our secret, we as authors 99% of the time go online and buy pictures/images of models for less than $5 bucks per image. These pictures/images are found at several websites. Here is a list of some of them:

www.123rf.com

www.photobucket.com

www.fotolia.com

www.graphicstock.com

www.istockphoto.com

www.fotosearch.com

These of course are just a few of them. There are many more but these are the ones that I normally use. As an author/writer each of these sites require you in most cases to join their group because each time you go to their site, you have to log in. The best thing about it is, their membership is free. However, each of these websites has a package plan of some sort. Example:

A starting package may cost $20.00 and you get 20 credits for that package. Each picture/image varies in cost/credits. In most cases, a picture/image that you might want to use for printing purposes will be anywhere from 3 to 5 credits. The reason is, for printing purposes, you will need a picture/image that's at least 300dpi. Please, please remember this…any picture/image you use, make sure it's 300dpi because your Graphic Artist will tell you that if you get anything lower than that, the picture/image will not pixel well on the cover of your book. In other words, your picture/image will look out of focus/or fuzzy looking.

Once you have chosen a picture/image, your Graphic Artist can take that image and place it in front of whatever back ground you prefer. Will your background be of a skyline, a beach, a bedroom, a club, a church? Again, in other words, your Graphic Artist can place your image in front of any background you choose.

Finding a Graphic Artist is easier than you think. As a brand, Graphic Artist advertize on social media sites as well. I will tell you, some Graphic Artist are better than others and the cost will vary depending on your need.

Most Graphic Artist will determine your cost based on whether you want a front cover (which are used for Ebooks) or whether you need a front cover, spine and back cover (which are used for Paperback books.)

The Right Way To Write Your Story

My own personal experiences with Graphic Artist and their cost have ranged anywhere from $50 to $250 dollars. Again, this depends on your needs. Needless to say, the cost will be cheaper if you just want a front cover for an Ebook. But, if you need the front, back and spine for your book, it will cost you more.

As I stated before, once you get into this game of being an author/writer, you will begin to meet other authors, Editors and Graphic Artist. Personally, after using several Graphic Artists for my books, I have chosen one to be my personal Graphic Artist and her name is Dominique Wilkens. In most cases, she can develop your book cover within 24 hours. For me, this is very important because I want to see my book cover come to life besides we always want something right then and there, that's just human nature. Also, I have found that Dominique's prices are the most reasonable out of all the other Graphic Artist that I have used.

I have asked Dominique if she mind that I post her information in this guidebook and she said, no, she didn't mind. So, here is her information:
www.AuthorDWilkensGOODbooks.com Email: AuthorDWilkens@gmail.com

This information basically is to get you started it doesn't mean you have to use the same Graphic Artist I use. But again, I will say, she is reasonable and fast.

Other Graphic Artist that I have used in the past charge a little bit more and there are times where it might take them more than a few days to complete your book. However, if you're like me, I want it now! That's just me but as the Author, it's your decision. Just beware because there are scam Artist out here and they will charge you an arm and a leg and take forever to do your book cover.

Chapter 6

Publisher vs. Self-publishing

This chapter will be the main focus of this handbook.

When I first started out back in 2005 writing my first book, "A Private Affair" I searched high and low looking for a publisher to publish my book. I didn't know any publishers and I didn't know any authors. I was clueless and didn't know where to turn.

I searched information on Publishers at the library as well as online but the information I found was not beneficial for me at all. I couldn't find one book or author that would tell me the truth about the publishing world. Well my friend, I'm going to give you the scoop. The truth as I know it to be.

When I found a publisher who was willing to give me a contract, I thought I had hit the lottery. I also thought that since a publisher would be willing to fork out the cost of an Editor, a Graphic Artist as well as have several thousand copies of my book produced, I thought I was the shit. Sorry for the language but it's the truth, my truth.

I also thought that I was better than a writer who had self-published their own book because they couldn't find a publisher to publish their book but I had. Little did I know that most small to medium size Publishing Companies take advantage of new writers/authors.

Here's the skinny, let's say that a small to medium size publishing company give you a contract for your book. What they will do is pay for everything up front, your book cover, a graphic artist, an editor and will have many copies of your book produce.

The Right Way To Write Your Story

Let's say your publishing company will charge $15 retail for the cost of your book, do you know how much of that you will get in royalties?

a. $10.00
b. $7.50
c. $5.00

Guess what, none of the above. If you're lucky you might get $2.00 in royalties for the sale of your book.

Surprise, don't be. Small to medium size Publishing Companies are like "Pimps" they will pimp you out like a prostitute and think nothing of it. Is that a harsh thing to say? Yes, but unfortunately, it's the truth. Most of these publishing companies don't want you to know that. So, beware and be armed because Publishing companies are out here to prey on new authors.

The only redeeming credit I can give to these Publishing Companies is, they can get your book out into the Masses. So, if you don't mind a publishing company taking more than 95% of the profits of your hard work and in exchange for getting your book and name out there, this may be the route you take.

I endured being "Pimped" for my first 4 books and even though my royalty checks sucked, they helped get my name out there and thus, I began to have a fan base. However, if I had to do it all over again and knowing what I know now, I would have published my own books from the very beginning and would have told my Publisher, "Go take a Hike."

Let me tell you why?

When you self publish you own the rights to your book. If you get a contract from a publishing company, they own the rights to your book. Hence, the publishing company can do whatever they want with your book as well as receive the majority of the profits from it.

You might not understand this now but as in all things, as the writer/author/creator of your book, (your baby) you need to have full control and say so when it comes to your work. Again, when you sign a contract from a Publisher, you sign all your rights away. I can't stress that enough.

I have had new authors hit me up online or call me and tell me about their horror stories about their Publisher's all the time. It's a sad situation but truth is Publishers take advantage of new writers all the time.

Self Publishing

I have self Published my last 4 or 5 books and I am so so so glad I did. Oh, did I mention how glad I am?

These books (my babies) give me full control and rights to everything. Yes, I had to fork out money for an Editor…$100.00 bucks….and yes, I had to fork out another $100.00 bucks for a Graphic Artist but, every book, every Ebook that is sold, I get all the profits from each sale.

I know becoming a new author/writer can be a little scary but this handbook/guide I hope will alleviate whatever fears you might have.

Let's say you have finished writing your manuscript, you've had sample readers read your manuscript, you hired an Editor, you have also hired a Graphic Artist and now you want to publish your own book. This is all you have to do:

Step one:

Go to: www.createspace.com you have to become a member and therefore will have to have a login name and password. Once you have done that.

Step two:

You have to fill out a questionnaire form that will ask for your name, your social security number (This is for the purpose of receiving royalties from you book(s), physical address, bank information (such as name of bank, routing number, bank acct number, etc…) again, this is for the purpose of receiving royalties directly deposited into your bank acct, you will need to complete a federal form number 9 and this is for the purpose of the IRS. You will also be asked what "Genre" your book is…Example: Romance, Hood Lit, Science Fiction, Urban Lit, etc…You will also be asked if your book is Fiction or Non-fiction…

The Right Way To Write Your Story

Step three:

Once you have completed the first 2 steps, now you will be asked to download a PDF copy of your manuscript. You might ask yourself, how do I turn my manuscript into a PDF file? Don't worry your Editor will email you a copy of your manuscript in a PDF format once they finish editing your book. This should only take a few minutes for it to download.

You will also be asked to price your book. Now, the cost of your Ebook and Paperback book is completely up to you. As a new author/writer you might only charge .99 cents for your Ebook and $5.99 for you paperback book. Again, this is up to you. Most new authors will charge these small amounts just so they can get a "Fan base." A Fan Base is exactly what it sounds like, a group of Readers that support your work.

Keep in mind, that as a new author/writer people don't know who you are and if you charge too much for your book, Readers may not buy it. For example, I know a new young author who wrote his first book and it was only 30 pages long and he charged $10.00 for his book. Other than family and friends, do you think he had a lot of sells? The answer is Hell NO!

So, as a new author/writer starting out and not having a fan base, you may not want to charge what well known authors charge. Like they say, you have to crawl before you walk. And in this case, you have to get a fan base before you can charge what other authors charge.

Step four:

Once you download your manuscript, the site will prompt you to take a look at what your book will look like. In other words, you will get a chance to review your manuscript in a book like format. It also will determine how short, how long and how many pages your book will have.

Step five:

After you review your manuscript in a book like format, now it is time for you to decide what size you want your book to be. In other words, how big or how small you want it to be. Examples:

1. 5x8
2. 5.5x8
3. 5.5x8.5
4. 6x9

And so on. The most popular size of a standard novel is 5.5x8.5of course the size of the book will also determine the page count of your book. The smaller size of your book will give you more pages. The larger size of your book will give you fewer pages. Does that make sense?

Once you have decided on the size of your book, you then have to download the cover of your book. Now, here is where it gets tricky. When you download your book cover, the book cover has to be within the "Red" borderlines. Example:

Here is your book  front cover, back cover and spine. Your book needs to fit into something like this:

This looks easy, but believe me when I tell you, it isn't. For me, this is the worse part of getting my book up online. Once you have your book within the parameter, you then have to submit all of this information all at one time. Just click on the submit button. Before you can get your book for sale online, Createspace will review it and if everything is within their guidelines, they will email you and let you know that your book is now available to be sold to the Masses. Trust me, this is a wonderful feeling to now be able to go online and see your book for sale.

However, I always seem to have a problem in doing this step and to be honest, I let my Graphic artist do this for me. Truth be told, I don't have the patience because once you think you have done everything right and to their guidelines, you have to wait 24 hours to see whether or not it does. And to get an email from Createspace telling you that it doesn't meet their guidelines, you have to download the cover of your book again and again, wait the 24 hour period to see if it's within their guidelines.

Let's say you received an email from Createspace and your book cover is within their guidelines...

Step six:

You are now ready to click the approve button that Createspace will give you and your book will immediately appear on their website: www.createspace.com

You will also be prompt to click on various book sites to have your book(s) for sale on those sites as well. The one thing I like about Createspace is that they work hand in hand with Amazon and your book will be ready for sale on Amazon immediately as well.

Once your book is online at Createspace you will have your own author's page. There, you can buy as many of your own paperback books as you like. For example: you've decided to charge $5.99 retail for your book, the cost to you may only be $3.00 bucks and in some cases it may be less than that...again, depending on how many pages your book has.

With an Ebook that cost .99 cents for the Masses it will also cost you .99 cents as well. But why would you want to buy and download your Ebook when you already have the PDF file for your book, anyway?

Most authors will buy several copies of their paperback novel to sale at a book signing, give it to family or friends or give to neighborhood book stores on an assignment bases.

This means, if there is a Ma & Pa book store in your neighborhood and you want that book store to carry your book. You might have 5 or more copies made and go to the book store, talk with the Owner/Manager and say, "My name is (Put your name here) and I'm a new author and here are copies of my new book, would you be willing to sale it on an assignment bases.

The Owner/Manager might say, "No I can't do that." However, if they say yes, generally, they will take a % of each book of yours that sells. The % will vary depending on the Owner or Manager of that store. But, whatever it may be, it's another way to get your book into a bookstore. So, it's still a win win for you as a new author.

Another reason most self publishing authors use Createspace is because it is a company that will print books on Demand, just like Amazon does. In other words, people can go on these sites and order your paperback book(s), they will mail them directly to the customer and this doesn't cost you a penny. How wonderful is that?

Companies that are Print on Demand basically are your own personal "Warehouse." Instead of you having to buy thousands of your own book(s) and then have to pay the cost of shipping your book out to a customer, these Print on Demand companies do it for you.

Before we get to the money (Royalties) let me say, another reason to use these Print on Demand websites is because they will also provide you with an **ISBN** number. You might ask yourself what is an ISBN number?

An ISBN number is a number that's used and placed on the back of your paperback book and every sell of that book is scanned for that ISBN number and that's how the book world and these Print on Demand companies keep track as to how many of your books are sold. The great thing about these Print on Demand websites is that your ISBN number is **FREE**.

But let's say you don't want to use any of these Print on Demand websites, you can actually pay for your own ISBN Number. A couple of these most popular sites for buying an ISBN numbers are:

www.bowker.com/products/ISBN-US.html

www.isbn-us.com

In most cases, these sites for buying an ISBN number is for Publishing Companies who have 5 or more authors in their company and the Publishing Companies want to allocate specific ISBN numbers to the books of their writers. Does that make sense?

Other than that, I really don't see a need for an author to buy their own ISBN number. For what, when you can get it for free? Again, paperback books are assigned ISBN numbers…I hope you understand that.

When it comes to Ebooks, they are assigned ASIN numbers and they too are **FREE**. Your Ebook is a book that a customer can download on the computer electronically off of Amazon or any other online book site. The ASIN number keeps track as to how many ebooks that have been electronically downloaded by customers.

With that being said, let's talk about **MONEY** and how and when you get paid. Let's say your book(s) are now posted online with Createspace and Amazon and today is May 12, 2015. Createspace and Amazon will hold back a month behind. Reason being, let's say someone buys your book on May 12, 2015 but on May 15, 2015 they decide they didn't like it and returned it. Createspace and Amazon will not pay you for return books.

Therefore, instead of getting royalty payments at the end of May, they will wait until the next full month 60 days (July) and will disburse your royalty payment on the 28th of July. All the sales you make for the month of June will be disbursed on August 28th, so forth and so on. In other words, there's almost a 2 month delay.

Let's say you don't have a bank account with a debit card attached to that account, Createspace and Amazon will mail you out a paper check on the 28th of each month. This means, you probably won't get it in the mail until 4 or so business

Mike Warren

days later. However, if you have a debit card attached to your bank account, they will deposit your royalties onto your card that same day.

You might ask yourself, what do Createspace and Amazon get out of being your "Warehouse" and mailing your books out for you? Well, they both will keep a small % of each book that is sold. Example: If the retail cost of your book is $5.99, both Createspace and Amazon will take a handling fee of $1.00 or maybe $2.00 at the most.

You might think that maybe that's too much, but if you consider buying your own books and shipping them out yourself, you will find that you will make out cheaper letting these books on Demand do it themselves and pay them the extra buck or two for doing it.

Also, once you get a fan base, you might have a fan of yours that might hit you up via facebook or by email and say, "Hey, how can I get an autograph copy of your book?" First off, thank them for wanting to buy your book. Secondly, let them know what your book cost and what it will cost you to mail it to them. Example:

Let's say your book sells for $5.99 and you want to mail an autograph copy of your book out to a customer. Always, always use "Media mail" because regardless of where your customer lives in the United States, the mailing fee is usually around $3 to $3.50. That is the cheapest rate for any book because if you send it out any other way, it will cost you based on the weight of your book. And sometimes, the weight of your book will cost you more to mail it than the actual cost of your book.

Therefore   book   cost: $5.99
Mailing cost: $3.50

Total cost………………………………………………………………………… $9.49

Now, as a writer you might tell your customer that in order to get an autograph copy of my book it will cost them $10.00, with this cost, you are just rounding everything off to the nearest dollar. Besides, even though you may charge a few pennies more, you still have to make the trip to the post office, right?

Chapter 7

Advertising

The only thing that I can say about this chapter is advertise your book wherever you go as well as online. Example: this is your book, If you enjoy playing around on facebook, Instagram or twitter, post your book as many times as you like on these sites. My favorite place to advertise is facebook, reason being, there are over 300 different book clubs on face book and you can post your book as many times as you like in these groups.

WARNING: Some of these book club groups have specific guidelines for authors posting their books. Please read these guidelines. The last thing you want to do is piss these book clubs off.

Also, please, please, buy as many **"Bookmarks"** as you can. Bookmarks are a great tool to advertise your book. Let's say you catch a train, bus, or subway each and every day back and forth to work. Leave some of your bookmarks behind. People who catch the subway, train or bus will see your bookmark and may like what they read and eventually may decide to buy your book online. One never knows.

Another trick in using bookmarks is, go to the library or to your favorite book store and check out the books that are in the same "Genre" as your book. Open them up and place your bookmark inside of other author's books. Example: Let's say you write Erotic novels and you know that Zane (Who is well known) writes nothing but Erotic novels, place one of your bookmarks in their book. There is nothing illegal about that. People who enjoy reading Erotic novels will see your bookmark and may decide to buy your book as well. And even though your book may not be on the bookshelf to purchase, the information on your bookmark should include the website as to where they can buy your book.

Also, there are so many radio shows and bloggers online that it will be your job as a new writer/author to reach out to them and let them know who you are and that you would love to be a "Spotlight Author" for their blog or radio show.

WARNING: Some of these bloggers/radio shows may charge you a fee for being a featured author on their show/blog but for a new author/writer this is not something new. As a new author, you sometimes have to pay people to get your name and book out there. As a new author, you have to decide if it's worth it.

Some of these bloggers/radio host will charge you anywhere from $50 bucks to $500 bucks, depending on what you want from them. Some of them will give you a featured package that includes the cover of your book, your bio, your website and where Readers can buy your book on their blog. Again, you have to decide whether this is beneficial for you or not.

Some bloggers/radio host won't charge you anything at all. You just have to be vigilant in searching out who these individuals are.

Another way to market yourself and your book is to check out the schools in your area, churches, Universities, certain groups in your neighborhood, don't be afraid to get your hustle on.

Another way to get your book out there is to have a **"Book Release Party."** Don't be afraid to have a party for yourself and invite family, friends, associates, neighbors, classmates, teachers, anybody and everybody to come and support your new baby (Your New Book.)

Again, advertise as much as you can wherever you are…Branding yourself and your book never stops, especially if you want a **FAN BASE**.

Chapter 8

Copyright Law:

Many new authors will ask, "Do I need a copyright for my book and where do I get it?" and what I always tell them, "As soon as you begin writing your book, there is already an assumption of copyright that your book receives automatically.

Most of them will look at me like I'm crazy because everybody knows that whatever you write you should protect it and file your application with the Library of Congress in order to copyright your material.

Before I became a professional writer, I too thought the same thing. However, like I said, when it comes to books, it's already an assumption of copyright when you begin writing your book.

When it comes to screenplays, sheet music, lyrics, movies, etc…that's a different story. You must file an application with the Library of Congress in Washington, DC. The address is: Library of Congress
101 Independence Ave SE.
Washington, DC 20540
Tel: (202) 707-5000

Below: I've attached the Copyright Basic Law to show that there is already an assumption of copyright law for your book:

Who Can Claim Copyright?

Copyright protection subsists from the time the work is created in fixed form. The copyright in the work of authorship immediately becomes the property of the author who created the work. Only the author or those deriving their rights through the author can rightfully claim copyright.

Now, with that being said, if you choose to still want to get your book/manuscript copyright you can. For book/manuscripts the fee is $35.00. There website for filing your manuscript/book is: www.copyright.gov

But, as I stated before, there's an automatic assumption already applied to your manuscript once you began to write it. The wording "In fixed form" basically means that you have written your manuscript on a recording device of some sort which also includes your laptop/computer. And to make it clearer, everything you write on your laptop/computer is being recorded just FYI. This alone is your proof of copyright if anybody ever wants to know.

Your basic copyright information that you will write in your book is this:

Copyright © Year

And these simple 2 paragraphs

All Rights Reserved. No part of this novel may be reproduced or transmitted in any form or by any means, electronic or mechanical, including photocopying, recording or by any information storage and retrieval system, without permission in writing from the copyright owner.

This is a work of fiction. Names, characters, places, and incidents either are the product of the author's imagination or are used fictitiously. Any resemblance to actual persons, living or dead, events, or locales is entirely coincidental and is in no way intended to be an actual account involving that person.

Copyright © "Year"

This is all you need to do when it comes to your copyright manuscript/book.

Chapter 9

The reality of being an author

Now that you have completed all of the above and now that your book is available for purchase. **DON'T QUIT YOUR DAY JOB.**

Many new authors assume that once they have published their book and it is now for sale, they think that they will become rich and famous. Not to burst your bubble but, **Ah, No**!

Believe it or not, there just a very small percentage of authors who can actually quit their job and earn a living off the sales of their book(s). I am happy to say, I am one of them.

But, this didn't happen overnight. I had been into this game for over 5 years before I could literarily quit my job and 9 published books later, 4 of which, I self published.

Truth of the matter is, it's going to take more than 3 or 4 self publish books of yours to even get to that point. Not to mention, it will take a lot of hard work on your part to continue to advertise your brand and your book.

If you think you're going to be a one hit wonder, think again. Now, if you just want to write one book and be done with it, that's up to you. However, let's say you do develop a "Fan Base" one of the first questions your fan will ask you, "When is your next book coming out?" How are you going to answer that question? This is just something for you to think about.

Being a writer/author there are many times you have to bite your tongue. Readers will talk about you and your book to the point, you feel like crying. The worst part is that you really can't say what you want to say because you don't want to piss that Reader off because if you do, trust and believe everybody they know and those that don't know you will hear about it. And that my friend will cause your book sales to drop.

Mike Warren

I remember when my first book came out, I was so excited, I could spit (lol). Anyway, I would check Amazon to see if anyone had read my book and whether or not they had written a review. And guess what? A young lady from a book club, I won't mention the name but she wrote a 4 paragraph review saying why she didn't like my book and gave it a one star (Which is the lowest a person can give) review.

I was so devastated that I had to leave work early and promised myself that I would never write another book. However, once I spoke to my publisher, she made me understand that bad publicity is almost as good as good publicity, if that makes sense? Meaning, someone was talking about my book and believe it or not, some Readers will buy a low rating book just to find out for themselves.

Once I understood the dynamics of publicity, I felt better about myself and my book. Thank God, I never gave up and neither should you. But remember, you have to have a "**Thick**" skin for being a brand because as we all know, there are a lot of haters out here.

So, in closing out this guidebook, I wish you the best of luck and if there is anything you need or that I can help you with concerning your book, please don't hesitate to contact me:

Mike Warren

One of The 2015 Kings of Literature

Email: becool031@gmail.com

https://www.facebook.com/mike.warren.986

Notes

Mike Warren

Notes

The Right Way To Write Your Story

Notes

Mike Warren

Notes